GW00889809

Meals for Older People

This book provides recipes for the main meat, fish and vegetarian dishes shown

in Anchor Homes' two weekly menus.

Also included are recipes for soups and salads, both cooked and raw, which may

be different from those found in the average cookery book.

Kathleen Bennett, aged 92, with her sixth great-grandchild. A Quaker vegetarian herself for 70 years, her family now has four generations of vegetarians.

Meals for Older People

Recipes with the health of the elderly in mind

Patricia Perry
**in conjunction with
Anchor Homes**

JON CARPENTER

Our books may be ordered from bookshops or (post free) from
Jon Carpenter Publishing, Alder House, Market Street, Charlbury,
England OX7 3PH
Credit card orders should be phoned or faxed to 01689 870437
or 01608 811969

First published in 2005 by
Jon Carpenter Publishing
Alder House, Market Street, Charlbury, Oxfordshire OX7 3PH
☎ 01608 811969

ISBN 0-9549727-1-6

Manufactured in England by LPPS Ltd, Wellingborough, Northants NN8 3PJ

Contents

Meat dishes

Fish dishes

Vegetarian dishes

Puddings

Breakfast, supper dishes and sauces

Introduction

This cookery book has been compiled for the use of all those who prepare meals for older people, either at home or in care and nursing homes. The cook, whether in the family or the chef in a nursing home, carries a heavy responsibility for the health of those he or she feeds. Our aim, therefore, has been to provide recipes which will aid and support the failing body and mind, but which also reduce and ease the time spent in preparation. Indeed, ease of preparation has been a particular goal in selecting menus suitable for those increasing occasions when meat and fish eaters sit down to eat at the same table as vegetarians.

Food is one of the pleasures of living, from babyhood until the end of life. For old people it is perhaps the most important social function of each day – and a great source of comfort. Aroma, flavour and appearance matter and we have therefore tried to create a balance between what will appeal to the senses and what is needed in terms of nutrition.

The recipes in this book are therefore designed to attract, to stimulate the circulation – important in keeping the brain active and in helping to heal sore and tender flesh – and to provide a good level of fibre. Fibre, together with enough oil, is essential to the prevention and control of constipation, especially when old people are no longer physically active. Constipation can have an effect on dementia, an unnecessary cause of suffering to both patient and carer. Constipation has also been known to affect cystitis, a miserable situation for old people.

Care of the elderly is demanding and stressful. Failing abilities, boredom, fear of death, loss of control over their lives and concern at the worse state of other old people around them (a particular problem in nursing homes) are all factors that intensify stress levels. Food that maintains the function of both mind and body at the best possible level helps to reduce stress and in doing so reduces stresses on both families and care staff too.

We would like to take this opportunity to pay a particular tribute to care and nursing home cooks. Their importance as members of staff is just as great at that of the nurses. In addition to being good cooks, they need to have an active interest in nutrition to ensure that the weekly menus they construct supply the dietary needs of the old people. In fact, they need to cook to the famous saying of Hippocrates, the father of modern medicine – **"Let food be your medicine and let medicine be your food"**. This excellent advice should be displayed on a large poster in the kitchen of every hospital, care and nursing home.

Patricia Perry
Charlbury 2005

WHOLEFOOD TRIAL WEEK ONE

	Sunday Lunch	Monday Lunch	Tuesday Lunch	Wed Lunch	Thursday Lunch	Friday Lunch	Saturday Lunch
	Roast beef & Yorkshire pudding	Salmon steaks with parsley sauce	Chicken casserole	Braised pork chops with apple sauce and gravy	Shepherds pie	Home-made battered cod with lemon	Liver & onion casserole
	Or	Or	Or	Or	Or	Or	Or
	Mixed nut roast with tomato sauce	Cheese and coriander pudding	Quorn pepper and shallot casserole	Aubergine and chickpea cous cous	Savoury pancakes with bean and mushroom stuffing and cheese sauce	Quorn and vegetable curry with rice	Cheese & vegetable quiche with parsnip & raisin salad
	Steamed spring greens, carrots	Broccoli, sauté courgette & celery seed	Buttered whole green beans, cauliflower	Braised green cabbage, swede	Sauté leeks with prunes, carrots	Peas, sauté spinach & ground cumin	Sprouts, Mediterranean oven roasted vegetables
	Roast potatoes in vegetable oil	New potatoes with mint	Baked potato,	Sauté potatoes	Parsley potatoes	Chips	Baked potato
	Coconut pudding with prune, apricot and orange sauce	Apple cake with crème fraiche	Brown rice pudding with apricots	Rhubarb and orange crumble & custard	Fruit salad with cream	Plum tart & custard	Dried fruit compote with yoghurt

	Sunday Supper	Monday Supper	Tuesday Supper	Wed Supper	Thursday Supper	Friday Supper	Saturday Supper
	Potato & celeriac soup with home-made bread	Watercress soup and home-made bread roll	Bean soup and home-made bread roll	Parsnip soup with home-made bread roll	Mixed vegetable soup with home-made bread roll	Sweetcorn chowder and home-made bread roll	Tomato soup & home-made bread roll
	Or	Or	Or	Or	Or	Or	Or
	Tomatoes on toast with raw cauliflower salad	Pasta salad with houmous and cucumber salad	Cheese onion and potato pie with sliced tomato and basil salad	Poached egg Florentine	Creamed mushrooms on toast and carrot mayonnaise	Potato, watercress & tomato with mixed fresh herbs & egg mayonnaise	Pasta salad and turnip salad with protein of your choice
	Salad of the day	Tomato quiche	Salad of the day	Salad of the day	Salad of the day	Salad of the day	Salad of the day
	Fresh fruit salad and cream	Peach melba	Cheesecake	Home-made banana ice-cream	Semolina pudding with jam.	Baked apples & crème fraiche	Blackforrest gateau and cream

Anchor
anchor homes

"In consultation with you, meals will be wholesome, appetising, enjoyable and satisfying".

This book provides recipes for the main meat, fish and vegetarian dishes listed in the Anchor Homes two weekly menus, shown above. Also included are recipes for soups and salads, both cooked and raw, which may be different from those found in the average cookery book. Some of

WHOLEFOOD TRIAL WEEK TWO

	Sunday	Monday	Tuesday	Wednesday	Thursday	Friday	Saturday
Lunch	Roast chicken with bread sauce, stuffing and gravy Or Spiced lentil loaf with mushroom sauce Roast parsnips, buttered green cabbage Roast potatoes Apple pie & custard	Beef bolognaise with pasta Or Cauliflower cheese Broad beans, carrots Mashed potato Baked banana and coconut pudding with hot rum sauce	Poached cod in tomato sauce Or Curried eggs with vegetables and brown rice Broccoli, sliced green beans Sauté lyonnaise potatoes Millet, apricot and prune pudding with coconut cream	Grilled lamb chops and mint sauce Or Vegemince bolognaise with pasta & carrot mayonnaise Spinach, sauté courgettes New minted potatoes Banoffi pie with cream	Steak & kidney pudding Or Millet and red pepper bake with tomato sauce Braised green cabbage, creamed turnips Mashed potatoes Fresh fruit salad and cream	Fresh battered haddock with lemon Or Parsnip savoury with mushroom sauce Peas, baked cauliflower Chips Jam & coconut sponge & custard	Beef & vegetable casserole Or Aubergine bake Sauté leeks, Brussels sprouts Oven baked potatoes Semolina with soaked figs
Supper	Beetroot soup & home-made bread roll & swirl of sour cream Or Cheese & chutney on toast with celeriac salad Salad of the day Fresh fruit salad and ice cream	French onion soup with cheese crouton Or Walnut pate & wholemeal melba toast with tomato and celery salad Salad of the day Chocolate roulade and cream	Celery soup with home-made bread roll Or Potato salad with mixed herbs, spring onions, watercress and houmous Salad of the day Queen of puddings with custard	Tomato soup with home-made bread roll Or Prawn cocktail salad or bean cocktail salad Salad of the day Strawberry shortcake	Carrot & coriander soup with home-made bread roll Or Rice salad, green salad and protein of your choice Salad of the day Mixed fruit crumble & custard	Lentil soup with home-made bread roll Or Scrambled egg on toast Salad of the day Profiteroles	Turnip soup with home-made bread roll Or Waldorf salad and vegetable pate or selection of meat or fish Salad of the day Mandarin cheesecake & cream

Anchor

"In consultation with you, meals will be wholesome, appetising, enjoyable and satisfying".

these include the use of celery, partly to enhance the taste of the dish, but also because celery provides fibre and is thought to be good for gout, rheumatism and kidney problems.

Portion sizes

The quantities given for meat and fish recipes are for 8–10 servings; all other recipes are for 4–6 servings.

Soups

Soups are one of the comfort foods, especially at the end of the day and especially for those who have reached the point where they cannot really be bothered to eat. It is therefore important that they should be at the right soothing texture and temperature, have a pleasant appealing flavour, and be nutritious.

We hope the following recipes fulfil these requirements.

BEAN SOUP

Beans are a source of protein. They also provide roughage and so aid constipation problems.

225g / 8 ozs red beans

1 red pepper, diced

1.2 litres / 2 pints vegetable stock

1 tablespoon tomato puree

2 cloves garlic, pressed

yeast extract and/or chilli powder

1 bay leaf

1 onion, diced

1 tablespoon chopped thyme

lemon juice

salt and black pepper

3 tablespoons vegetable oil

1.   Soak the beans overnight in just enough water to cover.

2.   Heat the oil in a soup pan and fry the diced onion and red pepper strips until they are soft.

3.   Drain the beans and add to the onion with the bay leaf, thyme and vegetable stock.

4.   Bring to the boil and simmer until the beans are cooked.

5.   Liquidise, return to the pan and add the tomato puree, salt, black pepper and lemon juice to taste.

6.   If liked, add a little yeast extract and/or chilli powder.

BEETROOT SOUP

Beetroot contains iron and so is helpful in cases of anaemia: it also soothes the nervous system.

2 medium beetroot

1 teaspoon anise seed

1.2 litres / 2 pints water

1 dessertspoon chopped thyme

1 head of celery

2 tablespoons barley flakes

soy sauce or yeast extract

yoghurt or sour cream

2 tablespoons olive oil

1 onion diced

1. Heat the olive oil in a soup pan and gently cook the diced onion until it is soft – about 2 minutes.

2. Add the diced celery and barley flakes, cover with 2 pints of water and bring to the boil. Boil gently for about 20 minutes.

3. Grate the beetroot and add to the pan with the anise and thyme. Boil gently for a further 15–20 minutes.

4. Liquidise, or strain through a sieve.

5. Reheat, add yeast extract or soy sauce and taste, adding salt if necessary.

6. Serve with a heaped teaspoon of full-cream yoghurt or sour cream.

CARROT AND CORIANDER SOUP

Carrots have many beneficial properties: they are rich in beta carotine which helps to improve vision, boost the immune system and improve overall health.

> 900g / 2 lbs carrots
> 1 onion
> 1 tablespoon oil
> 1.2 litres / 2 pints vegetable stock
> 1 bunch coriander leaves
> 1 medium potato

1. Heat the oil in a soup pan, slice the onion and cook gently in the oil until it is brown.

2. Add the scraped and sliced carrots, the peeled and diced potato and the stock and bring to the boil. Simmer until the vegetables are soft.

3. Liquidise then add salt, pepper and the chopped coriander leaves.

4. Place a small spoon of evaporated milk in each plate before serving.

CELERY SOUP

¶ Celery contains vitamins A, B and C and calcium and magnesium. It is thought to help problems with bones, joints, kidneys and bladder.

> 1 head of celery
> 25g / 1 oz butter
> 1 onion
> 1.5 litres / 2 ½ pints vegetable stock
> 2 tablespoons wholemeal flour
> 275ml / ½ pint milk
> parsley, thyme and celery seed
> cream or evaporated milk
> salt and pepper

1. Wash the celery, chop, and chop the onion.

2. Melt the butter in a soup pan, add the chopped celery, onion and one teaspoon of celery seed and cook gently until the vegetables are soft, stirring from time to time to prevent sticking.

3. Add the vegetable stock and simmer with the lid on for about 40 minutes, adding the herbs during the last 10 minutes.

4. Mix the wholemeal flour in a basin with the milk, add the soup to this, mixing carefully to avoid lumps, return to the soup pan and bring to the boil, stirring all the time.

5. Remove the thyme sprigs and liquidise.

6. Season with salt and pepper and, if necessary, add a small teaspoon of Vegemite.

7. Add a small spoon of cream or evaporated milk to each dish before serving.

SWEETCORN CHOWDER

Sweetcorn contains vitamins A, B and E and is said to be helpful in cases of gluten intolerance.

225g / 8 ozs sweetcorn (cooked and removed from the cob)

1.2 litres / 2 pints vegetable stock

1 tablespoon vegetable oil

1 clove garlic

2 medium potatoes

2 sticks celery, chopped

1 teaspoon celery salt

1 sliced onion

1 tablespoon chopped parsley

cream, or evaporated milk

salt, pepper, paprika .

1. Heat the oil in a soup pan, add the onions and pressed garlic and fry on a low heat for 2 minutes.

2. Add the chopped celery and raise the heat and cook for 5 minutes.

3. Add the vegetable stock, sweetcorn and potato and boil until tender.

4. Liquidise.

5. Reheat, add seasoning, cream or evaporated milk and chopped parsley before serving.

LENTIL AND WATERCRESS (OR SORREL) SOUP

Lentils are rich in protein and iron, are extremely nutritious and easy to digest.Watercress contains vitamins A, B, C and E. Like sorrel it stimulates the appetite and is helpful in dealing with winter colds and flu.

110g / 4 ozs Puy lentils

1.2 litres / 2 pints water

1 onion

1 large carrot

1 teaspoon grated lemon rind and juice of half a lemon

1 tablespoon oil or 1 oz butter

1 bay leaf

watercress or sorrel

1 vegetable stock cube, Vecon or Vegemite

salt and pepper

1. Soak the lentils overnight.

2. Heat the oil or butter in a soup pan , slice the onion and fry in the oil until golden,

3. Strain the lentils and add them with the 2 pints of water, the scraped and sliced carrot, the bay leaf and a handful of sorrel (if using sorrel instead of watercress) to the cooked onion. Bring to the boil and simmer for 30 minutes, or until the carrots and lentils are soft.

4. Remove the bay leaf, add the vegetable stock cube (or Vecon or Vegemite), the grated rind and juice of the lemon and liquidise.

5. Add salt and pepper to taste.

6. If using watercress instead of sorrel, chop it and add to the soup just before serving.

MUSHROOM SOUP

Mushrooms contain protein and so are useful in a vegetarian diet.

350g / 12 ozs mushrooms, sliced

1 oz wholemeal flour

1 onion, diced

chopped parsley

1 teaspoon Vegemite or soy sauce

evaporated milk

1 large clove garlic

50g / 2 ozs butter

1.2 litres / 2 pints vegetable stock

nutmeg

salt and pepper

1. Melt the butter in a soup pan, add the sliced onion and cook gently until golden brown.

2. Add the sliced mushrooms and garlic and cook gently for 2 minutes.

3. Remove from the heat, add the flour and mix well into the butter, followed by the vegetable stock , mixing thoroughly to avoid lumps.

4. Return to the heat, bring to the boil and simmer gently for 2 minutes, or until the mushrooms are cooked.

5. Liquidise, season, add grated nutmeg and sufficient evaporated milk to make a creamy consistency.

6. Serve sprinkled with chopped parsley.

ONION SOUP

Onions contain vitamins A, B and C. They are helpful to those with colds and catarrh and can benefit both the digestive and circulatory systems.

900g / 2 lbs onions

1.2 litres / 2 pints vegetable stock

pinch of mace

1 bay leaf

50g / 2 ozs butter

25g / 1 oz wholemeal flour

pinch of cayenne pepper

cream or evaporated milk

salt and pepper

1. Melt the butter in a soup pan, add the sliced onions and cook gently until brown.

2. Mix in the wholemeal flour and cook for a few seconds.

3. Remove from the heat, add the boiling stock together with the bay leaf, cayenne, mace and salt and simmer until cooked.

4. Serve with a little cream or evaporated milk.

PARSNIP SOUP WITH CINNAMON

Parsnip contains vitamins C, E , folic acid, fibre and minerals and is helpful for proper bowel function. Cinnamon helps the digestion and is used by some medical herbalists to treat colds and influenza.

450g / 1 lb peeled, chopped parsnips

1.2 litres / 2 pints milk (or milk and vegetable stock)

1 teaspoon cinnamon

50g / 2 ozs butter

2 bay leaves

salt and pepper

1. Melt the butter in a soup pan, add the parsnips and sweat gently until they are cooked.

2. Add the milk, or stock and milk mixed and liquidise.

3. Re-heat, add the cinnamon, salt and pepper and serve hot.

POTATO AND CELERIAC SOUP

A pleasant and comforting winter soup. The addition of rosemary stimulates the circulation.

900g / 2 lbs potatoes

2 tablespoons olive oil

I large celeriac

I onion, chopped

I tablespoon chopped rosemary

1.2 litres / 2 pints vegetable stock

cream or evaporated milk

salt and pepper

1. Fry the chopped onion in the olive oil until it begins to turn brown.

2. Peel the celeriac and potatoes and cut into 5cm / 2 inch pieces.

3. Add to the onion with the stock and simmer until tender.

4. Liquidise, reheat, add salt and pepper and serve with a sprinkle of chopped rosemary and a little cream or evaporated milk.

PUMPKIN SOUP

Pumpkin is rich in vitamin A and is recommended for those with intestinal problems such as constipation and colic. It has a calming and cooling effect and is helpful to ex and passive smokers.

450g / 1 lb chopped pumpkin, or squash

1 sliced onion

1.2 litres / 2 pints vegetable stock

2 tablespoons oil

2 heaped tablespoons tomato purée

rind and juice of half a lemon

1 celery heart, chopped (or celeriac)

chopped parsley

soy sauce or Vegemite

1 bay leaf

salt and pepper

1. Heat the oil in a soup pan and cook the sliced onion with a bay leaf until the onion is soft.

2. Add the chopped celery or celeriac, and cook on a high heat for 3 or 4 minutes.

3. Add the pumpkin and the heated stock, bring to the boil and simmer until both pumpkin and celery are soft.

4. Remove the bay leaf, add the tomato purée, Vegemite and rind and juice of the lemon.

5. Liquidise.

6. Season and serve with chopped parsley.

TOMATO SOUP

Tomatoes contain vitamins A, B and C and help to stimulate the appetite. They are thought to help conditions such as arteriosclerosis, vascular disorders, arthritis and bladder and gall stones.

2 tins tomato juice

1 onion, sliced

1 head of celery or celeriac, finely chopped

single cream or evaporated milk

1 large clove garlic

fresh basil, coriander, tarragon, or parsley

2 tablespoons oil

570ml / 1 pint water

1 tablespoon tomato puree

1 vegetable stock cube

1. Heat the oil in a soup pan and cook the sliced onion until it is soft and brown.

2. Add the crushed garlic, tomato juice, water, celery or celeriac and stock cube.

3. Bring to the boil and cook until tender.

4. Liquidise, ensuring that the celery is assimilated into the liquid.

5. Add salt and pepper.

6. Place a little cream or evaporated milk in each plate before serving and sprinkle with chopped herbs.

CREAM OF TURNIP SOUP

Young turnips are best for this as the flavour does not want to be too strong.

> 900g / 2lbs turnips
>
> I finely sliced onion
>
> 25g / I oz butter
>
> mixed spice
>
> 1.2 litres / 2 pints mild vegetable stock
>
> milk, salt and pepper

1. Melt the butter in a saucepan, add the onion and cook gently until golden.

2. Wash and scrape the turnips, where necessary, and slice them.

3. Add the turnips to the cooked onion and cook gently for about 5 minutes

4. Add the vegetable stock, bring to the boil and boil until the turnips are soft.

5. Liquidise the cooked turnips and onion, adding the spice, salt and pepper and enough milk to make a thin and drinkable consistency.

MIXED VEGETABLE SOUP

This soup can be liquidised when cooked if a smooth consistency is needed.

1 large onion, finely sliced

1 pepper, de-seeded and diced

450g / 1 lb potatoes, peeled and sliced, or 450g / 1 lb parsnip, peeled and sliced

25g / 1 oz barley flakes (optional)

1 leek, cleaned and sliced

450g / 1 lb carrots scraped and sliced

1 tablespoon tomato purée

2 tablespoons vegetable oil

1.2 litres / 2 pints vegetable stock

2 tablespoons chopped fresh herbs

salt and pepper

Vecon or Vegemite to taste

1. Heat the oil in a soup pan and fry the onion until it is soft.

2. Add the chopped and sliced vegetables (and barley flakes if using them) the heated vegetable stock and boil gently until all the vegetables are tender.

3. Add the tomato purée, salt and pepper and Vecon if needed.

4. Serve with a sprinkle of chopped fresh herbs in each plate.

WATERCRESS SOUP

Watercress contains vitamins A, C and E as well as iron, iodine and phosphorous. It is said to be good for lack of energy, to aid digestion and to stimulate the circulation.

1 bunch watercress, finely chopped

450g / 1 lb potatoes

1 medium onion, chopped

1.2 litres / 2 pints vegetable stock

1 tablespoon vegetable oil

salt and pepper

cream, or evaporated milk

Vegemite or Vecon if needed

freshly grated nutmeg

1. Heat the oil in a soup pan, add the onions and cook gently until they are soft.

2. Peel the potatoes, dice and add to the onion with the 2 pints of boiling stock.

3. Cook until the potatoes are tender, then liquidise.

4. Add salt, pepper and freshly grated nutmeg to taste, and the finely chopped watercress. Add Vecon if needed, and finally the cream or evaporated milk.

Salads

Salads are an essential component of a healthy diet for young and old alike. Apart from the fact that uncooked food has a richer content of vitamins and trace elements than its cooked counterpart, salads stimulate the processes of elimination and are therefore particularly important for the elderly who quickly suffer from constipation as their bodies function ever more sluggishly.

Unfortunately, old people find salads difficult to eat and digest and one sees the sad sight of waste in homes as lettuce, tomatoes and cucumber are returned to the kitchen at the end of the meal. The following recipes are therefore suggested to help overcome the problem both for the caterer and the old person.

However, it should be understood that root vegetables grated by the mechanical graters used in commercial kitchens are not suitable for old people. The successful acceptance of the following recipes therefore depends on the use of fine hand graters.

But cooked salads too are a good way of helping the elderly to eat chopped raw green leaves and vegetables such as celery. It is easier to eat spring onions, watercress, lettuce hearts, herbs and celery when they are finely chopped and mixed with, for example, cooked potato, pasta, couscous, bulgar wheat, cooked beans and lentils and cooked cauliflower.

BEAN OR CHICK PEA SALAD

Beans and chick peas are a good source of fibre as well as protein.

I tin of kidney or mixed beans or chick peas
I small onion, finely chopped
2 tomatoes skinned and chopped
I red pepper
I tablespoon grated celeriac or chopped celery
I tablespoon chopped parsley
I tablespoon vinaigrette
lemon juice

1. Grill the pepper until the skin is black on all sides, then skin and dice. Add a little lemon juice and leave the pepper to stand for about 1 hour.

2. Skin and chop the tomatoes.

3. Mix all the ingredients together, cover and leave to stand for 2 or 3 hours to allow the beans to absorb the juices from the vegetables and parsley.

BEETROOT SALAD

Beetroot contains vitamins A, B and C, and is a source of natural sugar. It also contains important minerals, such as iron.

I medium beetroot

I tablespoon cream, crème fraiche or yoghurt

I tablespoon orange juice

chopped coriander, dill and/or snipped chives

1. Wash and scrape the beetroot and grate finely.

2. Add the cream, orange juice and herbs and mix thoroughly.

CABBAGE OR COLESLAW SALAD

Cabbage contains vitamins A, B, C, K and E. It is thought to help reduce the risk of bowel cancer, cardiovascular disease and digestive ailments.

> 1 small head of hard-centred white cabbage
>
> 1 teaspoon celery seeds
>
> 1 tablespoon onion, grated on a fine grater
>
> 2 tablespoons mayonnaise
>
> 1 tablespoon sultanas and/or 1 tablespoon grated carrot
>
> chopped parsley and/or other herbs such as lovage

1. Wash the cabbage and slice very finely.

2. Cover with boiling water and allow to stand for 5 minutes. Then strain.

3. When cool add the grated onion and other ingredients and mix well. A skinned, chopped tomato can be added in place of the carrot.

CARROT MAYONNAISE

Carrots are very easy to digest and are said to be helpful in the treatment of constipation. The addition of orange or lemon juice, which contain vitamin C, is thought to help the body absorb the iron in the carrot. Freshly grated root ginger has been found to stimulate the circulation.

110g / 4 ozs carrots

1 tablespoon mayonnaise

1 teaspoon finely grated root ginger

juice of half a lemon or orange

1 dessertspoon raisins

1. Wash the carrots and scrape them, rinsing well under running water.

2. Grate on a fine grater.

3. Mix the ginger into the mayonnaise and add to the grated carrots with the remaining ingredients.

CAULIFLOWER SALAD

Cauliflower belongs to the cruciferous family of plants and possesses the same anti-cancer properties as cabbage: it is particularly protective against colon cancer due to its sulphurous components.

I small cauliflower

juice of half a lemon

2 tablespoons mayonnaise

chopped parsley or snipped chives

1. Remove the outer leaves of the cauliflower and discard. Wash the cauliflower.

2. Grate the cauliflower very finely.

3. Add the remaining ingredients and mix well.

Variations on this recipe include: adding finely milled walnuts, raisins, or skinned, chopped tomato, or chopped mint and orange as an alternative to parsley and chives.

CELERIAC SALAD

Celeriac contains vitamins A, B and C and can help to lower levels of blood cholesterol.

I large celeriac

juice of half a lemon

2 tablespoons live yoghurt, or fresh double cream.

1. Wash and peel the celeriac.

2. Grate finely.

3. Add the remaining ingredients and mix thoroughly.

COUSCOUS SALAD

Couscous is a great source of carbohydrate and will provide slow releasing energy for the day. The chick peas or beans are a good source of fibre as well as providing protein.

> 225g / 8 ozs couscous
>
> 1 tablespoon chopped onion, or spring onion
>
> 1 chopped roasted red pepper
>
> 1 tin chick peas, or 1 tin beans
>
> 4 tablespoons olive oil
>
> 2 peeled and seeded tomatoes
>
> chopped parsley or coriander
>
> salt, pepper and brown sugar
>
> 570ml / 1 pint boiling water
>
> 1 teaspoon soy sauce.

1.   Add the soy sauce to the boiling water.

2.   Mix the couscous into the boiling water, cover, remove from the heat and leave to stand until the water has been absorbed and the couscous is cool.

3.   Make a vinaigrette with the olive oil, lemon juice, salt, pepper and brown sugar.

4.   Add the remaining ingredients to the cooled couscous with the vinaigrette and mix well.

Variations include substituting bulgar wheat for the couscous. Chopped cucumber and mint make an interesting alternative to the parsley and chopped tomatoes.

CUCUMBER SALAD

Cucumbers contain vitamins A, B and C and are recommended in salads for people with constipation. They should not be peeled as the peel contains some of their beneficial properties. Unlike other raw vegetables which should be grated on very fine graters, the whole cucumber should be grated on a coarse grater, which softens the flesh and makes it easy to eat: finely grated cucumber quickly turns to juice.

> 1 cucumber
>
> 1 tablespoon creme fraiche, live yoghurt or cream.
>
> 1 dessertspoon fresh chopped mint, dill, or watercress

1. Wash the cucumber and grate on a coarse grater.

2. Add the remaining ingredients and mix well.

MILLET SALAD

With the exception of oats, millet contains more vitamins than any other grain. It helps to control the cholesterol levels in the blood and can be useful in dealing with nerve problems and arteriosclerosis.

225g / 8 ozs millet grain

2 tablespoons vinaigrette

110g / 4 ozs dried soaked apricots

1 tablespoon finely chopped onion

1 tablespoon olive oil

chopped coriander or parsley

orange or apple juice

1. Soak the apricots in the apple or orange juice.

2   Gently fry the millet grains in the olive oil until the grains begin to turn a pale brown.

3. Add boiling water to the millet and cook gently for about 30 minutes until soft.

4. Drain and allow to cool.

5. Add the remaining ingredients to the cooled millet and mix thoroughly.

PARSNIP AND RAISIN SALAD

Parsnip is sweet when eaten raw. The addition of cinnamon, which is regarded by health practitioners as a natural antiseptic, enhances the flavour.

110g / 4 ozs raw parsnip

1 tablespoon mayonnaise or natural yoghurt

½ teaspoon cinnamon

juice of ½ an orange or orange slices

1 tablespoon raisins

1.   Wash and scrape or peel the parsnip and grate on a fine grater.

2.   Add the cinnamon to the mayonnaise.

3.   Add the rest of the ingredients to the parsnip and mix all together.

As an alternative to the cinnamon add finely chopped watercress.

PASTA SALAD

Like bread, pasta contains complex (slow assimilation) sugars and a fair amount of protein. Pasta salads are an easy way for older people to eat raw foods and herbs.

175g / 6 ozs fusilli, macaroni or penne (preferably wholemeal)

2 tablespoons mayonnaise

1 tablespoon finely chopped onion or 1 clove of garlic

4 sticks finely chopped celery

2 skinned chopped tomatoes

chopped watercress or mixed fresh herbs

tinned or roasted red pepper, chopped

lovage leaves, celery salt and pepper

1. Cook the pasta, strain and cool.

2. Add the onion to the mayonnaise and mix this into the pasta with the remaining ingredients.

3. If it is acceptable, a clove of garlic (either very finely chopped or put through a garlic press) can be used instead of the onion.

POTATO SALAD

Peeled potatoes lose many of their vitamins and minerals in the boiling process. It is preferable, therefore, to boil them in their skins, and to remove the skins when the potato is cold. This is also a great way to get people to eat celery or watercress.

> 450g / 1lb old or new potatoes
>
> 1 tablespoon chopped onion or spring onions
>
> 2 skinned chopped tomatoes
>
> chopped mixed herbs, watercress, or celery
>
> mayonnaise or vinaigrette
>
> salt and pepper

1.   Wash the potatoes and boil in their skins until soft enough to slice.

2.   Strain and allow to cool.

3.   Slice the potatoes – the peel can be left on if acceptable.

4.   Add the remaining ingredients and mix well.

RICE SALAD

Wholegrain rice contains vitamins A and B, fibre and protein and is an energy-giving food that helps to lower blood pressure and avoid diarrhoea. Brown basmati rice is suggested for this dish.

225g / 8 ozs washed brown rice

I tablespoon chopped onion

25g / I oz sultanas soaked in orange juice

2 tablespoons vinaigrette

2 tablespoons finely chopped celery

chopped mixed fresh herbs

grated rind of I orange or I lemon

salt and pepper

1. Cook the rice, strain and cool.

2. Add the remaining ingredients to the cold rice and mix well.

3. Season to taste and serve with cooked or raw salads.

TOMATO SALAD

Tomatoes are rich in vitamins A and C and fibre. They stimulate bowel movement, facilitate the digestion of starch and help such conditions as vascular disorders, arthritis, gout, rheumatism and bladder problems.

> **6 tomatoes**
> I clove of garlic
> vinaigrette
> basil leaves or chives
> salt and pepper

1. Scald, skin and slice the tomatoes.

2. Press the garlic and add to the vinaigrette.

3. Cover the tomatoes with the vinaigrette and top with torn basil leaves or finely cut chives.

4. If the vinaigrette lacks salt and pepper, add a little more before serving.

TURNIP SALAD

Turnips and swedes belong to the cruciferous family of vegetables and possess the same anti-carcinogenic properties as cabbage.

110g / 4 ozs turnip

1 tablespoon vinaigrette dressing

1 tomato, skinned and sliced

basil or parsley

1. Wash and either scrape or peel the turnip.

2. Grate finely.

3. Cover the grated turnip with the sliced tomato.

4. Pour the vinaigrette over the turnip and tomato and top with torn basil leaves or chopped parsley.

5. Cover and allow to stand for 1 hour, during which time the tomato juices will seep into the turnip, thereby enhancing the flavour of the dish.

WALDORF SALAD

Walnuts are thought to help lower cholesterol and to be good for the circulation.

1 head of celery

1 large sweet apple

50g / 2 ozs walnuts

50g / 2 ozs chopped dates

1 small chopped onion

mayonnaise

1. Remove the outer stalks of the celery – these can be reserved for stock. Chop the remainder finely, add the peeled, chopped apple and the chopped walnuts and onion.

2. Mix well together with a tablespoonful of mayonnaise.

HUMMUS

Chick peas contain iron and magnesium. They are easy to digest and are helpful to those with poor digestions.

    1 tin chick peas
    4 tablespoons tahini
    3 cloves garlic
    rind and juice of 1 or 2 lemons
    salt and pepper
    paprika
    olives, chopped red pepper, or chopped herbs

1. Drain the water from the chick peas, reserving it to thin the final result if needed.

2. Add the tahini, crushed garlic, rind and juice of 1 lemon and liquidise.

3. Season with salt and pepper. If necessary add more lemon and/or water from the tinned chick peas.

4. Serve with olives or sliced red peppers, sprigs of watercress and/or herbs, and either toast or biscuits.

PEANUT BUTTER DRESSING

Peanuts are rich in iron, protein and fat and this dressing is a good way to add calories.

75g / 3 oz peanut butter

juice of 1 lemon

1 teaspoon soy sauce

1 teaspoon brown sugar

tabasco sauce or cayenne pepper to taste

Put all the ingredients into the liquidiser and liquidise until creamy.

• This dressing goes particularly well with the pasta, rice or millet salads (see pages 38, 40 and 42) when it can be used instead of vinaigrette.

Meat dishes

The following meat dishes, which are included in the two Weekly Menus shown on pages 10 and 11, are good examples of the main meals offered each day in Anchor Homes. In addition, we have tried to make sure that each day's food, whether for meat/fish eaters or for vegetarians, supplies a good nutritional balance by including raw salads and dishes made with wholegrains and brown sugar.

We hope that in this way the diet will provide the variety and fibre needed to keep the body in good health and that this combination will be enjoyed by everyone.

BEEF BOLOGNAISE

850g / 1 lb 14 ozs minced beef

55ml / 2 fl.ozs tomato puree

55ml / 2 fl.ozs red wine

2 sticks fresh celery

2 lbs tinned chopped tomatoes

55ml / 2 fl.ozs vegetable oil

3 cloves garlic

225g / 8 ozs onions

50g / 2 ozs carrots

3 ozs beef stock

½ grated nutmeg

basil

salt & pepper, and water if needed

1. Finely chop the onion, celery, carrot and garlic.

2. Heat the oil in a pan, fry the onion and garlic for 1 minute and then add the carrots and celery and continue to fry on a low heat until soft.

3. Add the beef mince, stirring well to break it down. Cook until the mince has changed colour.

4. Add the nutmeg and tomato puree and cook for a further 2 minutes.

5. Add the tomatoes, beef stock and red wine. Bring to the boil, reduce the heat and simmer for 1 to 1½ hours.

6. Correct the consistency with a little water if needed and season as required.

7. Serve with cooked pasta.

BEEF AND VEGETABLE CASSEROLE

2 tablespoons sunflower oil

900g / 2 lbs steak cut into 25mm / 1 inch cubes

2 rashers streaky bacon cut in strips

1 large onion

6 sticks of celery

225g / 8 ozs carrots

2 cloves of garlic, crushed

40g / 1 ½ ozs plain flour

150ml / ¼ pint beef stock

150ml / ¼ pint red wine

1 tin tomatoes

thyme and parsley

1. Heat the oil in a flame-proof casserole. Add the beef and bacon and cook over a moderate heat for 3 minutes until browned on all sides. Remove with slotted spoon and drain.

2. Slice the onion and add to the pan cooking gently until soft.

3. Remove the pan from the heat, stir in the flour, add tomatoes, stock and red wine.

4. Return the meat to the casserole, add the chopped celery, the sliced carrot, crushed garlic, thyme, salt and pepper and bring to the boil.

5. Cover the casserole and place in the oven at 160 C. (325 F, Gas 3) for about 2 hours, or until the beef is tender.

6. Add parsley to serve.

7. Cauliflower florets, sliced green peppers and/or potatoes can be added to this dish.

ROAST BEEF

1400g / 3 lbs topside of beef

dripping or oil

1. Heat the oven to 230-250°C/450-500°F/Gas 8-9.

2. Season the joint with salt and place on a trivet on a roasting try.

3. Place a little dripping or oil over the top of the joint and place the roasting tray in the heated oven.

4. Baste frequently and reduce the heat gradually when necessary. Roasting time is 15 minutes per 500g /1 lb and 15 minutes over.

5. Beef is normally cooked underdone at which point a little blood should show in the juice. To test if cooked enough (i.e. according to the taste of the customers) place on a tray and press firmly to see if the juices contain any blood.

6. When done, remove the tray from the oven and allow the joint to rest for 15–20 minutes. This allows the meat to set and facilitates carving.

7. Carve against the grain.

8. Allow 75g/3 ozs per portion and serve the slices moistened with a little gravy, yorkshire pudding and a little watercress.

9. Serve sauceboats of gravy and horseradish sauce separately.

Parsnips can be peeled, cut in half and added to the roasting tray about 40 minutes before the joint is cooked.

GRILLED LAMB CHOPS

10 x 150g / 5 ozs lamb loin chops

vegetable oil

salt and pepper

1. Place chops on a rack, season and lightly oil.

2. Cook quickly to the required degree.

3. Garnish and serve immediately accompanied by mint sauce, peas and halved grilled tomatoes.

LIVER AND ONION CASSEROLE

450g / 1 lb calf's liver, cut into strips

1 large onion, sliced

110g / 4 ozs streaky bacon, in strips

450g / 1 lb carrots, sliced

2 tablespoons sunflower oil

3 tablespoons tomato purée

chopped parsley

salt and pepper

570ml / 1 pint beef stock

2 tablespoons plain flour

1. Heat the oil in a large flame-proof casserole, add the onion and bacon and cook gently.

2. Add the liver and cook for 2–3 minutes, stirring all the time.

3. Add the carrots, mix together and remove the contents from the casserole.

4. Put 2 tablespoons of plain flour into the casserole, gradually add 1 pint of beef stock, heat to boiling point, stirring until it thickens.

5. Add tomato purée and season.

6. Return liver, bacon and carrots to the casserole, cover and cook in a moderate oven for about 40 minutes.

BRAISED PORK CHOPS

5 boneless pork chops

1 large onion, chopped

100g / 4 ozs sliced mushrooms

1 clove garlic, crushed

4 chopped tomatoes

150 ml / ¼ pint white wine

2 tablespoons chopped parsley

1 teaspoon basil

1 teaspoon coriander

1 teaspoon cornflour

salt and pepper

2 tablespoons vegetable oil

1. Heat half the oil in a pan and sauté the onion for 5 minutes. Add the mushrooms and garlic, then sauté for a further 5 minutes. Stir in the tomatoes and parsley and cook for one minute.

2. Add wine, basil, coriander, cornflour (mixed with a little water) and seasoning. Cover and simmer 15 minutes.

3. Heat remaining oil in a frying pan and fry chops on both sides for 15 minutes. Cover with sauce and braise for 10 minutes.

4. Serve with chopped parsley.

SHEPHERD'S PIE

900g / 2 lbs potatoes

1 onion, chopped

450g / 1 lb minced beef or lamb

1 red pepper, sliced

220ml / 8 fl. oz beef stock

1 tablespoon plain flour

1 clove garlic, crushed

1 tablespoon vegetable oil

1 tsp chopped parsley

3 tablespoons milk

75g / 3 ozs grated cheddar cheese

nutmeg

salt and pepper

knob of butter

1. Cut potatoes into even sized pieces. Cook in a pan of seasoned water until tender. Drain.

2. Sweat the onions in a large frying pan for 3-4 minutes.

3. Add the mince, garlic and red pepper and cook for 5 minutes. Stir in the flour, add the stock and bring to the boil, stirring continuously.

4. Mash the potatoes and mix with milk and butter. Season.

5. Spoon mince into an ovenproof dish, top with potato, sprinkle with cheese and bake for 30 minutes at 200°C/400°F/Gas 6.

STEAK AND KIDNEY PUDDING

700g / 1½ lbs rump steak
225g / 8 ozs ox kidney
2 chopped onions
thyme and marjoram
2 tsp soy sauce
2 tablespoons port
beef stock
butter and seasoned flour
  Suet crust:
350g / 12 ozs plain flour
175g / 6 ozs grated suet
4 teaspoons baking powder
1 teaspoon salt, black pepper

1. Trim excess fat from the meat and kidney and toss in seasoned flour.

2. Butter a 500ml / ¾ pint pudding bowl.

3. For the suet crust, sift the flour, baking powder and salt into a bowl. Add black pepper and suet. Stir in about 12 tablespoons cold water to make a soft dough.

4. Knead the dough and roll out into a round large enough to line the bowl. Cut out enough of the circle to make a lid, line the bowl with the remainder and place the meats in the lined bowl, adding the chopped onion and herbs.

5. Pour the soy sauce and port over the meat and cover with the suet crust lid.

6. Cover the pudding with a buttered sheet of greaseproof paper, pleated down the centre to allow the pudding to rise. Cover with foil and tie firmly in position with string.

7. Steam the pudding, covered, for 4–5 hours.

8. When cooked, cut a small hole in the top of the pudding and pour in a little rich beef stock.

9. Serve the pudding in its bowl, wrapped in a clean napkin, accompanied by a green vegetable.

ROAST STUFFED CHICKEN

225g / 8 ozs bacon
50g / 2 ozs oil
I bay leaf
I chopped onion
sprig of thyme
275ml I ½ pint brown stock
25g / I oz wholemeal breadcrumbs
I 10g / 4 ozs butter
juice of half a lemon
225g / 8 ozs chicken livers (optional)
I tbsp tomato purée
I chicken (1.5 kg / 3 lbs)

1.   Prepare the stuffing by cutting the bacon in small pieces.

2   Fry off quickly in a frying pan with the oil, herbs and chopped onion for a few seconds.

3.   Add the trimmed chicken livers if using them.

4.   Season and fry quickly until brown. Add the tomato purée.

5.   Clean, prepare, season and truss the chicken.

6.   Fill the chicken with the prepared stuffing and roast at 220°C/425°F/Gas 7 for 20 minutes. Then reduce to 180°C/350°F/Gas 4 for a further 25 minutes or until the chicken is cooked.

7.   If pot roasting, remove the lid half way through to get a brown colour.

8.   When cooked, remove the string, place the chicken on a flat serving dish and keep warm.

10.   Remove the fat from the cooking dish, deglaze with brown stock and lightly thicken with a little diluted arrowroot. Pass through a fine sieve and serve separately.

12.   Cook the butter in a frying pan to a beurre noisette, mix in the breadcrumbs and lemon juice and pour over the chicken.

13.   Sprinkle with chopped parsley and serve with bread sauce.

CHICKEN CASSEROLE

4 chicken quarters

1 medium sized onion

845ml / 1 ½ pints chicken stock

4 tablespoons plain flour

3 bay leaves

1 teaspoon caster sugar

50g / 2 ozs butter

1 lemon

1 tablespoon oil

salt and pepper

50g / 2 ozs streaky bacon

1. Halve the chicken quarters and season well with salt and pepper.

2 Heat the butter and oil in a frying pan and fry the joints until golden brown on all sides. Transfer to a casserole.

3. Slice the onion and lemon. Place the onion in the frying pan with the bacon and cook until tender. Mix in the flour and cook for 1 minute.

4. Blend in the stock and bring to the boil stirring all the time.

5. Add the sliced lemon, bay leaves, sugar, salt and pepper and pour into the casserole.

6. Cook at 190°C / 375°F/ Gas mark 5 for about 1 hour, removing the casserole lid 5 minutes before cooking ends.

Fish dishes

An increasing number of people today prefer to eat fish rather than meat. The following fish dishes together with the vegetarian options – all listed on the Weekly Menus – should provide the choices that people want.

BATTERED COD

700g / 1½ lbs cod steaks

110g / 4 ozs self-raising flour

3 beaten eggs

1 tablsp. chopped parsley

½ pint milk

salt and pepper

1. To make the batter sift the flour into a bowl, add the beaten eggs and a little milk, and blend to a smooth paste.

2. Whisk in the remaining milk and leave to stand for 15 minutes.

3. Place the cod steaks in an oiled dish in a pre-heated oven at 200°C/400°F/Gas 6 for 5 minutes until the flesh is soft and flakes from the bone.

4. Add the batter and bake for a further 15–20 minutes.

POACHED COD
WITH TOMATO AND GARLIC

450g / 1 lb cod steaks

1 small onion

1 tablespoon olive oil

350g / 12 ozs tomatoes

1 clove garlic

150ml / ¼ pint white wine

150ml / ¼ pint fish stock

50g / 2 ozs butter

parsley

salt and pepper

1. Wash the cod and place in a buttered ovenproof dish.

2. Slice the onion and cook in the oil until soft but not brown.

3. Add the onion, the skinned, deseeded and sliced tomatoes, chopped garlic and parsley to the fish.

4. Pour the wine and fish stock over the cod and season with salt.

5. Cover the dish with buttered paper, bring to the boil over a moderate heat and poach gently.

6. Remove the cod and drain.

7. Reduce the cooking liquid, mix in the butter, season as necessary and add chopped parsley.

8. Pour the cooking liquid over the cod and serve on a bed of creamed potatoes and grilled mushrooms.

BATTERED HADDOCK

700g / 1 ½ lbs haddock fillet, skinned

110g / 4 ozs flour

275ml / ½ pint milk

3 beaten eggs

grated nutmeg

salt and pepper

1. Lightly butter a shallow ovenproof dish.

2. Cut the haddock into 3 pieces and place in the dish in a single layer.

3. Sprinkle with salt and pepper.

4. Bake at 230°C/450°F/Gas 8 for a few minutes until the flesh is soft. Remove from the oven.

4. Make the batter by sifting the flour into a bowl. Gradually mix in the beaten eggs and a little of the milk. Add half a grated nutmeg. Blend to a smooth paste and whisk in the remaining milk.

5. Leave to stand for 10 minutes.

6. Pour the batter mixture over the haddock and cook for another 20 minutes.

7. Serve with slices of lemon.

GRILLED SALMON STEAKS WITH PARSLEY SAUCE

10 slices of salmon 1½ in / 4cm thick

seasoned flour for coating

salt and pepper

oil for greasing

sprigs of parsley

1. Pass the salmon steaks through seasoned flour. Shake off all surplus flour.

2. Place the steaks on a greased baking sheet, or grill bars, and brush with oil.

3. Grill on both sides for about 10 minutes, brushing frequently with oil.

4. Remove the centre bone and garnish with sprigs of parsley.

5. Serve with white wine and cream sauce.

Vegetarian dishes

Cooks wonder what they can prepare for the vegetarian, how they can replace the meat or fish dish with something acceptable to the non-meat eater: an omelette, macaroni cheese, a vegetable lasagne, quiche and salad – and then what? If one is working from the normal ingredients and recipes of the meat/fish kitchen then variety in the menu and establishing a nutritional balance becomes an issue.

Variety in the menu is not really difficult if one turns to the peasant dishes of the world and finds the delicious recipes of North Africa, the Middle East, France, Italy, Greece, India and the Far East.

However, nutritional balance is more of a problem because a straight forward substition of the meat dish by cheese or eggs does not in itself mean that the exchange will guarantee the vegetarian the same vitamins, trace elements, etc. that were present in the meat dish. The vegetarian diet depends on finding nutrients in all the constituents of the meal and it is therefore important that vegetarian dishes, including puddings and cakes and biscuits, are made with wholegrain cereals, wholegrain pasta and brown sugar.

The ingredients of the vegetarian kitchen include a wide variety of beans, peas, lentils, oils (olive, sesame, groundnut, coconut, sunflower, grapeseed, walnut – all of which carry distinct flavours and have special uses), herbs, spices, nuts, seeds, fruits and vegetables, seaweeds, soya products, different grains (barley, buckwheat, corn, millet, oats, rice, rye and wheat), brown sugar and dairy products such as yoghurt, soft cheese, eggs, milk, butter, cream and cheese made with vegetarian rennet.

AUBERGINE BAKE

❢ Aubergine contains minerals and vitamins A and B. It is thought to be beneficial to the kidneys and nerves.

450g / 1 lb aubergines
1 large onion
225g / 8 ozs tomatoes
2 cloves garlic
2 cooked potatoes, sliced for topping
1 egg
4 tablespoons yoghurt
3 tablespoons oil
2 tablespoons grated cooking cheese
salt and pepper
chopped coriander
wholemeal flour

1. Wash and slice the aubergine, cover both sides with salt, cover, place a weight on top and leave to stand for 1 hour, at which point each slice can be dried and wiped with a paper cloth.

2. Dip the aubergines in wholemeal flour, heat the oil in a frying pan and fry the aubergines to a golden brown on both sides. Place the aubergine slices in a shallow pie dish.

3. Remove from the pan and fry the sliced onion in the remaining oil. When cooked, add the skinned sliced tomatoes and chopped garlic to the onion and cook till soft.

4. Beat the egg, add it to the yoghurt with salt and pepper.

5. Pour this mixture over the aubergine slices, top with sliced potato followed by grated cheese.

6. Cook in the oven at 190°C/375°F/Gas 5 for about 25 minutes, until the top is browned and crisp.

7. Serve with a tomato sauce, baked potatoes and a green vegetable.

AUBERGINE AND CHICK PEA COUSCOUS

A very satisfying dish. The chick peas contain magnesium and potassium in addition to vitamins A and B.

1 aubergine

1 onion

1 green pepper

1 courgette

1 tin chick peas

2 tablespoons oil

1 large tomato

50g / 2 ozs raisins

1 tablespoon tomato paste

1 carrot

1 teaspoon yellow mustard seeds

1 teaspoon paprika

1 clove garlic

salt and pepper

pinch cayenne pepper

parsley or coriander

1. Heat the oil in a frying pan and fry mustard seeds, cayenne and paprika for 1 minute. Add the chopped onion and chopped garlic and cook gently until golden.

2. Add the chopped aubergine, peppers, carrot, courgette and the raisins and cook with the lid on until tender. Add the chick peas.

3. Finally add the chopped tomato and tomato paste.

4. Season as necessary with salt and pepper and add the chopped herbs.

5. Serve on a bed of couscous.

CAULIFLOWER CHEESE

Cauliflower is an alkaline vegetable so may help those suffering from acidity.

I medium sized cauliflower

110g / 4 ozs grated cheese

4 tablespoons brown breadcrumbs

¼ pint white sauce

cayenne pepper

salt

1. Break the cauliflower into florets, wash and steam for 10–12 minutes until just tender.

2. Turn into an ovenproof dish and cover with sauce and brown breadcrumbs.

3. Top with grated cheese and heat under the grill until the cheese turns golden brown.

4. Sprinkle very lightly with cayenne pepper and serve.

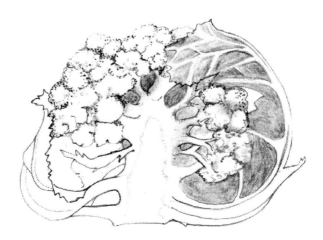

CHEESE AND VEGETABLE QUICHE

A useful, attractive-looking dish that can be made in quantity and frozen for later use.

110g / 4 ozs wholewheat flour, <u>or</u>
50g / 2 ozs white flour and 50g / 2 ozs wholemeal flour
50g / 2 ozs vegetable fat (e.g. Trex)
2 eggs
570ml / 1 pint milk
110g / 4 ozs grated cheese
2 tablespoons cold water
selection of vegetables, sliced, tinned, or cooked
1 tomato (optional)
salt and black pepper

1. Sift the flour into a bowl with the salt

2. Add the fat and mix with the fingers until the mixture looks like breadcrumbs.

3. Mix to a dough with the cold water and refrigerate for 1 hour to chill.

4. Line a shallow round pie dish with the pastry and prick the base with a fork.

5. Beat the eggs into the milk, add salt and black pepper and pour into the flan case.

6. Add vegetables – e.g. sliced courgette, peppers, carrots, tinned beans, chick peas, or broad beans.

7. Sprinkle grated cheese evenly over the top of the flan and place in the oven at 190°C/375°F/Gas 5 for 30-40 minutes.

8   If liked, sliced tomato can be added 5 minutes before removing the flan from the oven.

9. Serve topped with chopped parsley.

CHEESE AND CORIANDER PUDDING

Coriander has an interesting flavour and has medicinal characteristics which are said to help the digestive system.

I small onion

110g / 4 ozs grated cheddar cheese

I teaspoon French mustard

110g / 4 ozs wholemeal breadcrumbs

2 free-range eggs

150ml / ¼ pint milk

chopped coriander

salt and pepper

1. Peel the onion and chop roughly.

2. Place all the ingredients, with the exception of the cheese, into the liquidiser and blend until smooth.

3. Add the cheese to the blended mixture and place in a greased, shallow baking dish. Bake at 200°C/400°F/Gas 6 for 45 minutes until set and golden on top.

4. Sprinkle the top of the pudding with the chopped coriander and serve. If no fresh coriander is available use parsley.

CHEESE, ONION AND POTATO PIE

The use of rosemary, which aids the circulation, enhances the flavour of this dish.

> 1 large onion, chopped
>
> 2 large potatoes (approx 600g / 1 1/4 lbs)
>
> 75g / 3 ozs grated cheese
>
> 1 bay leaf
>
> 1 tablespoon chopped rosemary
>
> 1 tablespoon oil
>
> salt and pepper

1. Scrub the potatoes (do not peel them) and cook until firm but not too soft.

2. Peel and slice the potatoes.

3. Fry the chopped onion in oil with the bay leaf until soft and golden.

4. Place layers of sliced potatoes, rosemary, fried onion and grated cheese in a shallow pan, ending with a layer of cheese.

5. Season with salt and pepper.

6. Bake in a moderate oven 180°C/350°F/Gas 4 for about 25 minutes, and then brown quickly under the grill.

EGG CURRY WITH BROWN RICE

When served with brown rice and dahl, this provides a warming and satisfying meal.

> 8 hard-boiled eggs
> 1–2 teaspoons curry powder
> 4 tablespoons melted butter
> coriander leaves
> 4 large tomatoes
> 1 onion, finely sliced

1. Heat the butter in a saucepan and gently fry the finely sliced onion.

2. Stir in the salt, the skinned chopped tomatoes and chopped coriander leaves and simmer gently until the sauce begins to thicken a little.

3. It may be necessary to add a little lemon juice depending on the ripeness of the tomatoes.

4. Add the halved eggs and heat through gently.

5. Serve with brown rice, either plain or curried vegetables and dahl.

SPICED LENTIL LOAF

Lentils are rich in minerals, low in fat, and a good source of protein.

½ lb puy lentils

1 chopped onion

2 cloves garlic, pressed

2 eggs

4 ozs brown breadcrumbs

2 bay leaves

2 tablespoons tomato puree

rind of a lemon

2 teaspoons sesame seeds

juice of ½ lemon

1 teaspoon cumin seeds

1 teaspoon Vegemite

1 teaspoon coriander seeds

salt and pepper

1 tablespoon oil

1. Soak the lentils in enough water to cover for one hour. Strain, add fresh water and cook until soft.

2   Fry the onion in oil with the bay leaves until they are soft and golden.

3. Grind the spices and fry with the cooked onion for half a minute.

4. Add the Vegemite to the lentils, which should have absorbed most of the water in which they were cooked..

5. Add the onion and spices to the lentil mixture together with the Vegemite and the remaining ingredients, mix well and put the mixture into a greased loaf tin.

6. Bake in a moderate oven 180°C/350°F/Gas 4 for 30 minutes.

7. Serve with a tomato sauce.

MILLET AND RED PEPPER BAKE

¶¶ Millet is useful for those on a gluten-free diet. It also helps to balance the nervous system.

225g / 8 ozs millet grain
570ml / I pint milk and water
I bay leaf
I chopped onion
2 eggs
I tablespoon olive oil
I tablespoon grated cheese
I tablespoon tomato paste
I tablespoon chopped thyme
oil for frying
I red pepper
salt and pepper

1.   Fry the chopped onion in the oil until it becomes golden brown.

2.   Add the millet grain and cook with the fried onion for about I minute until the grain begins to turn brown, stirring all the time to avoid burning. Remove from the heat.

3.   Meanwhile brown the red pepper under the grill. When blackened all over remove the skin and cut into thin strips.

4.   Heat the milk and water, add to the browned millet and bring to the boil. Simmer until the millet is dry and fluffy, adding a little more water if needed.

5.   Remove from the heat, add the beaten eggs, chopped thyme, tomato paste, red pepper strips, salt and pepper. Mix well.

6   Place in a greased pie dish, top with grated cheese and cook in the oven at 190°C/375°F/Gas 5 for 8–10 minutes.

7.   Serve hot with a red pepper and tomato sauce, or cold, cut into slices and fried.

MIXED NUT ROAST

Nuts are a good source of protein and contain vitamin B. Other herbs may be used in place of sage and thyme.

225g / 8 ozs mixed nuts (brazils, cashews, walnuts)

110g / 4 ozs soaked brown bread

1 dessertspoon salted, roasted peanuts

1 beaten egg

1 tablespoon chopped sage and thyme

1 onion

1 tablespoon vegetable oil

1 tablespoon bran

tomato juice to mix

salt and pepper

1 teaspoon Vegemite

1. Chop the onion and fry gently in the oil until browned.

2. Grind the nuts until they are like breadcrumbs. Add them to the soaked brown bread with the beaten egg, the bran and the herbs and the teaspoon of Vegemite melted in a little hot water.

3. Add sufficient tomato juice to make a soft but firm mixture.

4. Season with salt and pepper and bake in a greased loaf tin at 200°C/400°F/Gas 6 for about 35 minutes.

5. Serve hot with vegetables and a tomato or mushroom sauce, or cold with salads.

PARSNIP SAVOURY

Parsnips have small amounts of essential oils, vitamins C and E, phosphorus and potassium.

> 2 large parsnips
> 2 medium sized onions
> I small tin evaporated milk
> I beaten egg
> ½ teaspoon aniseed
> celery salt
> paprika
> I tablespoon olive oil

1. Scrub the parsnips and either bake in the oven, or boil until tender.

2. Braise the sliced onions in the olive oil.

3. Mix the braised onions with the boiled or baked parsnips, the egg beaten with a little evaporated milk, aniseed, celery salt and paprika and liquidise.

4. Bake in a greased pie dish for about 30 minutes at 190°C/375°F/Gas 5.

5. Serve with mushroom sauce, fried potatoes and a green vegetable.

QUORN, PEPPER AND SHALLOT CASSEROLE

Quorn, low in fat and a good source of fibre, is made from fungi, egg white and roasted barley.

175g / 6 ozs Quorn nuggets

2 tablespoons oil

110g / 4 ozs shallots

1 tin tomatoes

1 red pepper

1 green pepper

coriander and parsley

2 sticks celery

1 bay leaf

salt and pepper

1. Heat the oil in a shallow pan, peel the shallots and cook them in the oil with a bay leaf for about 2 minutes.

2. Add the chopped peppers and chopped celery to the shallots in the frying pan and continue cooking gently until the celery is soft.

3. Add the tin of tomatoes and bring to the boil.

4. Add the Quorn nuggets to the shallots, pepper and celery and cook gently until the volume of liquid is slightly reduced.

5. Add salt and pepper and chopped herbs.

6. If liked, this dish can be cooked in a casserole in the oven once the shallots, pepper and celery have been slightly cooked in the shallow pan.

QUORN AND VEGETABLE CURRY

¶ A teaspoon of coriander seeds, crushed in a pestle and mortar, can be added to this dish.

175g / 6 ozs Quorn nuggets, or Quorn mince
175g / 6 ozs frozen peas
1 cauliflower
450g /1 lb carrots
1 tin tomatoes
1 tablespoon oil
25g / 1 oz butter
1 bay leaf
1 tablespoon curry powder
275ml / 10 fl.ozs vegetable stock
fresh coriander
salt

1. Heat the butter and oil in a saucepan and fry the chopped onion until golden. Add the Quorn, bay leaf and curry powder and fry gently.

2. Stir in the sliced carrots and cauliflower florets, the tinned tomatoes and juice, the vegetable stock and the frozen peas.

3. Bring to the boil and simmer until the vegetables are tender.

4. Add salt as necessary and serve with brown rice.

TOMATO AND CHEDDAR QUICHE

Tomato helps prevent the formation of uric acid and reduces inflamation of the digestive tract.

> 275g / 10 ozs short pastry (half wholemeal/half white flour)
>
> 60g / 2½ ozs grated Cheddar cheese
>
> 2 eggs
>
> 300 ml milk
>
> 4 tomatoes
>
> cayenne pepper, salt

1. Slice the tomatoes thinly.

2. Line a flan dish with a thin lining of pastry and prick the bottom with a fork.

3. Cook in a hot oven at 230°-250°C/450°-490°F/Gas 9 for 3-4 minutes until lightly set.

4. Remove from the oven, press the pastry down if it has risen slightly and add the tomato slices and the cheese.

5. Beat the eggs into the milk, add salt and cayenne pepper and pour into the flan dish.

6. Return to the oven and cook at 200°-230°C/400°-450 °F/Gas 6–8 and bake for about 20 minutes until nicely browned and set.

7. Serve, hot or cold, with a sprinkle of chopped parsley or basil leaves.

VEGEMINCE BOLOGNAISE

Vegemince is made from the soya bean, which contains protein, vitamins A and B, and minerals.

6 ozs Vegemince or Quornmince

1 tablespoon oil

1 onion

1 can tomatoes

2 cloves garlic

4 sticks celery

1 green pepper

chopped herbs

1 tablespoon tomato paste

salt and pepper

1.   Heat the oil in a saucepan and add the sliced onion, chopped celery and sliced green pepper.

2.   Cook gently until the onion browns and the vegetables are soft.

3.   Add the chopped garlic and can of tomatoes and cook for about 1 minute.

4.   Add the Vegemince and salt and pepper and cook for 2 minutes.

5.   If necessary, add one teaspooon Vegemite to enhance the flavour.

LENTIL AND TOMATO SAUCE

This can be used instead of the Vegemince Bolognaise, or as a sauce with pasta. It can be frozen for future use.

4 ozs / 110g puy lentils

350ml / 10 fl ozs water

1 onion

1 tablespoon oil

1 red pepper

1 clove garlic, grated

1 bay leaf

1 teaspoon Vecon

4 tablespoons tomato purée

350ml / 10 fl ozs vegetable stock

lemon juice

freshly ground black pepper

salt

1. Chop the onion and fry in the oil with the bay leaf.

2. Meanwhile boil the lentils separately in the water, simmering for about 30 minutes. Cook the pepper under the grill until the skin blackens and can be removed. Chop the red pepper.

3. Add the cooked lentils, red pepper, grated garlic, Vecon, tomato purée, vegetable stock, salt and pepper to the onion. Place this in the liquidiser and liquidise for 30 seconds. Add lemon juice to taste before serving.

STUFFING FOR PANCAKES

¶ Mushrooms contain potassium, sodium and sulphur and some vitamin B. The chick peas in this recipe can be replaced by tinned red kidney beans.

I small onion

I dessertspoon oil

I tablespoon tinned chick peas

I tablespoon tomato purée

4 large flat mushrooms

I teaspoon butter

I teaspoon brown sugar

grated nutmeg

salt and pepper

1. Slice the onion finely.

2. Melt the butter with the oil in a frying pan, add the sliced onion and cook slowly until it is golden and soft.

3. Slice the mushrooms and add to the cooked onion.

4. Add salt and grated nutmeg to the onion and mushroom, cover and cook slowly on a medium heat for about 1 minute.

5. Add the tomato purée and the chick peas with a sprinkling of brown sugar and heat gently.

6. Stuff wholemeal pancakes with this mixture and serve.

Puddings

Most puddings are made with white flour, white sugar and white rice and they are deliciously sweet and most acceptable to the elderly. The following recipes, however, use wholemeal flour, brown sugar and unpolished rice and so have the advantage of additional vitamins and mineral salts. We hope that they too will be found to be deliciously sweet and, most importantly, that they will also aid the process of elimination.

APPLE CAKE PUDDING

Can be eaten hot or cold. It keeps well for 3 or 4 days.

225g / 8 ozs wholemeal self-raising flour
110g / 4 ozs margarine
1 teaspoon cinnamon
110g / 4 ozs brown sugar
1 teaspoon mixed spice
275g / 10 ozs peeled and cored apples
75g / 3 ozs chopped dates, raisins or sultanas
1 beaten egg
rind and juice of 1 lemon

1. Grease an oblong tin (approx. 18x25cms/7x10 ins) and line with greaseproof paper.

2. Sift flour and spices into a mixing bowl.

3. Add the brown sugar and mix in with the fingers to remove any lumps.

4. Add the margarine and rub in until the mixture resembles fine crumb.

5. Cut the apples into small pieces and add to the mixture with the grated lemon rind and juice and the dried fruit.

6. Finally mix in the beaten egg.

7. Spread evenly into the lined tin and bake in the oven at 190°C/375°F/Gas 5 for 45 minutes.

8. Cool in the tin. Cut into squares for serving.

9. Serve with cream, full fat yoghurt or crème fraiche.

This is an adaptation of a Cranks recipe for Devon Apple Cake.

BAKED BANANA AND COCONUT PUDDING

Bananas have mild antibacterial properties but are not always good for diabetics.

6 medium ripe bananas

75g / 3 ozs desiccated coconut

2 tablespoons butter

25g / 1 oz brown sugar

100 ml / 4 fl.oz orange juice

rum

1. Peel the bananas and cut in half lengthways.

2. Arrange in layers in a generously buttered baking dish.

3. Mix the orange juice and brown sugar and pour over the bananas.

4. Dot the bananas with the remaining butter and top with the coconut.

5. Bake in a hot oven until the bananas are softened and the coconut turns golden brown.

6. Pour over a little rum before serving.

BANANA AND COCONUT ICE CREAM

🍴 Coconut contains natural sugars and protein. Bananas have vitamins A, B and E and mineral salts but are sometimes unsuitable for diabetics.

> **3 good sized bananas**
> **rind and juice of 2 limes**
> **275ml / ½ pint double cream**
> **6 tablespoons coconut powder**
> **3 tablespoons brown sugar**

1. Put the lime juice, grated peel and bananas in the liquidiser.

2. Liquidise, then add the sugar and coconut powder and switch on again for 5 seconds.

3. Beat the cream until it is stiff.

4. Add the beaten cream to the banana mixture and transfer to a freezer tray (or use an ice cream maker).

5. If appropriate a spoonful of fresh coconut can be added to this mixture before it is frozen, or the ice cream can be served topped with coconut – though this may make it too chewy for some people.

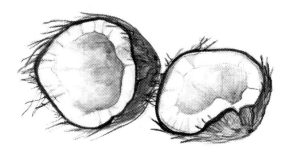

COCONUT PUDDING

This pudding should help combat constipation.

50g / 2 ozs creamed coconut fat

50g / 2 ozs brown sugar

110g / 4 ozs desiccated coconut

grated rind of 1 lemon

1 egg, separated

25g / 1 oz wholemeal flour

25g / 1 oz dates

110g / 4ozs dried prunes, apricots and/or other fruit, soaked

juice of 1 orange

1. Beat the creamed coconut and brown sugar together until soft.

2. Add the egg yolk and lemon rind, then fold in the sifted flour, followed by the coconut.

3. Beat the egg white until stiff and then fold into the mixture.

4. Turn the mixture into a greased shallow tin, top with chopped dates and bake in the oven at 200°C/400°F/Gas 6 for 30 minutes.

5. Liquidise the soaked dried fruit. Add the orange juice and a little of the water used for soaking the fruit.

6. Warm this sauce through gently and serve with the pudding.

FRUIT CRUMBLE

For use with apples, plums, gooseberries, rhubarb or mixed soft fruit.

> 225g / 8 ozs plain wholemeal flour
> 110g / 4 ozs margarine
> 50g / 2 ozs brown sugar
> 50g / 2 ozs rolled oats
> 900g / 2 lbs fruit sweetened with 50g–75g / 2ozs–3ozs brown sugar

1. Sift the flour into a mixing bowl and rub in the margarine and brown sugar.

2. Add the rolled oats and mix well.

3. Prepare the fruit, sweeten accordingly with brown sugar and place in a pie dish.

4. Sprinkle about half the crumble mixture evenly over the top, pressing down to form a firm seal. The remainder can be frozen.

5. Bake in a moderate oven for 15–30 minutes depending on the fruit.

6. If liked, a little sugar can be sprinkled over the top and caramelised under the grill.

MILLET, APRICOT AND PRUNE PUDDING

Millet contains iron, magnesium, fibre and protein and is helpful for those who need a gluten free diet. This recipe is also useful for those who need sugar-free puddings.

> 50g / 2 ozs millet flakes
> 1 orange
> 110g / 4 ozs mixed apricots, prunes & dates
> 275ml / 10 ozs water

1. Chop the fruit and soak in just enough water to cover for about 1 hour.

2. Bring to the boil and cook for 2 minutes.

3. Put the millet flakes in a saucepan, add the water, mix well and bring gently to the boil, stirring all the time to ensure that it does not stick.

4. Put the soaked, boiled fruit and the cooked millet into the liquidiser, together with any water remaining after the fruit has been cooked, and liquidise.

5. Add the rind and juice of the orange.

6. Serve with coconut cream, or creme fraiche.

BROWN RICE PUDDING WITH DRIED APRICOTS

Rice is suitable for those on a gluten-free diet. Brown, unpolished rice should be used: polished rice loses most of its important ingredients. This dish is good for the digestive system.

40g / 1½ ozs brown rice

25g / 1 oz dried apricots

850ml / 1½ pints milk

1 tablespoon brown sugar

1. Soak the apricots for 2–3 hours in just enough water to cover. When soaked chop them thoroughly.

2. Wash the rice, drain and place in an ovenproof pie dish with the milk and the soaked chopped apricots. If this will not be sweet enough add a tablespoon of brown sugar.

3. Heat the oven to 140°C/275°F/Gas 1. Place the dish in the oven and cook for about 2–2½ hours. Stir the mixture half way through the cooking period and again just before the end.

4. Serve with a little evaporated milk, or coconut cream.

Other recipes ...

KATHLEEN BENNETT'S GRANOLA

¶ This is a good anti-constipation food, to be eaten with other cereals at breakfast time. It should be crisp when baked in the oven and not too difficult to eat. It also contains many useful minerals and vitamins.

5 cups rolled oats

1 cup soya flour

1 cup ground nuts

1 cup desiccated coconut

1 cup wheat germ

1 cup sesame seeds

1 cup sunflower oil

1 cup sunflower seeds

1 cup honey, or 1 cup raisins

1 tablespoon blackstrap molasses

1. Mix all the ingredients together in a mixing bowl, with the exception of the raisins. measuring the oil in the cup before measuring the honey. It is helpful to mix the ingredients together as one would for pastry.

2. Turn into a baking tin and cook at 180°C/350°F/Gas 4 for about 40 minutes, turning the mixture over several times to ensure that it browns evenly. It should be crisp when cooked.

3. Cool, then add a cup of raisins and pack into an airtight container.

Note: A cup of wheat flakes, rye and/or barley can be added to this recipe.

MEXICAN EGGS

Chillis contain capsaicin, believed to help the heart and circulation.

4–6 eggs
1 onion
2 tablespoons olive oil
half a small red chilli
1 tin tomatoes
salt and brown sugar

1. Slice the onion.

2. Remove all the seeds from the chilli and chop into really small pieces.

3. Heat 1 tablespoon of oil in a frying pan, add the onion and chopped chilli and cook gently until the onion begins to turn brown.

4. Add the tinned tomatoes, including the juice, to the onion and cook over a high heat until the tomato is reduced to a thick sauce. Add salt and if necessary a little brown sugar.

5. Heat the remaining oil in a separate pan and fry the eggs.

6. Serve the eggs on toast topped with the tomato sauce.

MUSHROOM SAUCE

Mushrooms may be useful in strengthening the immune system. This sauce goes well with cereal dishes as well as pasta.

50g / 2 ozs mushrooms

nutmeg to taste

1 shallot or small onion

25g / 1 oz wholemeal flour

1 teaspoon chopped herbs

570ml / 1 pint vegetable stock

1 ½ tablespoons cream or

30g / 1 ¼ ozs butter

evaporated milk

salt and pepper

1.　Wash and chop the mushrooms and the shallot.

2.　Melt half the butter in a saucepan, add the chopped shallot and cook briskly for about 1 minute.

3.　Then add the mushrooms, a grating of nutmeg, salt and pepper and cook gently for about 3 minutes.

4.　Add the remaining butter, remove from the heat and stir in the flour.

5.　Add the stock, mixing thoroughly to avoid lumps, and return to the heat, stirring until the mixture boils and thickens.

6.　Remove from the heat, add the cream and the herbs and test for flavour, adding more salt and pepper and nutmeg if necessary.

MUESLI

This breakfast or supper dish is easy to eat and digest, a good way for older people (and children) to eat fresh fruit, and an excellent source of trace elements and vitamins. It is an adaptation of Dr. Bircher-Benner's muesli, used in his clinic in Zurich and eaten all over Switzerland.

3 tablespoons oat flakes

3 grated apples

1 sliced banana

1 tablespoon honey

3 tablespoons live yoghurt

1 tablespoon chopped dates

1 tablespoon raisins or sultanas

1 tablespoon ground almonds

any other fresh fruit in season

1. Soak the oat flakes overnight in just sufficient water to cover.

2. In the morning add the unpeeled grated apples and all the remaining ingredients.

3. Mix well and serve cold.

WALNUT PATÉ

Walnuts have a mild laxative effect and can be helpful in lowering cholesterol. They contain vitamins A, B and C, iron and magnesium. They need to be ground finely for this recipe, which works well with crème fraiche.

> 225g / 8 ozs walnuts
>
> 7 ozs / 200g double cream or crème fraiche
>
> I large clove garlic
>
> 2 tablespoons chopped parsley
>
> lemon juice to taste
>
> salt and black pepper

1. Grind the walnuts to a fine consistency.

2. Whip the double cream, or use the crème fraiche straight from the tub, and add to the walnuts with the pressed garlic and chopped parsley.

3. Season with the lemon juice, salt and black pepper.

BANANA YOGHURT

This dish is delicious, sustaining and very easy to eat when one is feeling tired, poorly or totally disinterested in food. It is also a marvellously easy way to keep the bowel functioning properly.

> 1 banana
> 3 tablespoons full cream live yoghurt
> 1 teaspoon honey
> 1 tablespoon other soft fruit (such as strawberries, peaches, plums, greengages, ripe pears, melon etc.; or soaked cooked dried fruit such as prunes or apricots)

1. Mash the banana thoroughly, add the yoghurt and honey and mix well. Mash the other soft fruit and add to the dish.

Serve for breakfast or supper, or as a pudding.